D0594396

GRACES for TODAY

GRACES
for
TODAY

Compiled by Susan Skinner

John Hunt
Publishing Limited

PREFACE

A Grace book, by definition, recognizes the free and open gift of God's grace.

This small book reaches out, however, not only to believers, but to people who may not define themselves as religious, yet who are open to the spirit and to the power of words.

Although these Graces are mostly drawn from the great Christian tradition, they are all directed to the present time, to life as we lead it. Every day we make unexpected discoveries about ourselves and the world around us. Likewise, in a spirit of serendipity, I have not categorized these Graces. They are to dip into whenever you need the comfort of words that show us we are not alone and that our private joys and sorrows, irritations and minor triumphs, have been and always will be, common to humankind.

A prayer mat is a small rug on which people kneel and prostrate themselves during prayer. In this book each Grace has its own minute prayer mat on which you may, perhaps, imaginatively, kneel down and rest your spirit for a while.

ACKNOWLEDGEMENTS

I would like to thank all my friends who gave me their favourite Graces or wrote their own; the Oxford University Press for permission to use prayers from The Oxford Book of Prayer, edited by George Appleton (1985) and for all those whom I have been unsuccessful in contacting.

DEDICATION

To Jo Lintott whose spirit touched us all.

A GRACE FOR THOSE WHO PART

May the road rise to meet you.
May the wind be always at your back.
May the sun shine warm upon your face.
May the rains fall softly upon your fields
Until we meet again
May God hold you in the hollow of his hand.

A GRACE FOR PEACE

Deep peace of the Running Wave to you.
Deep peace of the Flowing Air to you.
Deep peace of the Quiet Earth to you.
Deep peace of the Shining Stars to you.
Deep peace of the Son of Peace to you.

A GRACE BEFORE NATURE

May the great rhythms of the natural world -
Winter's meditation, spring's unfurling,
Summer's flourish, autumn's grave procession,
Pulsing tides, the silent ordering
Of snow and petal, leaf and starlight, bind us
To Nature's constancy and renovation,
So our worn hearts may beat to Nature's heart
No longer lost but cradled by creation.

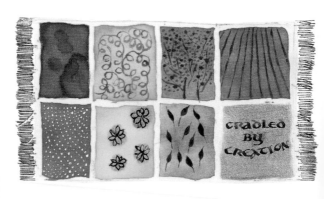

A GRACE FOR NATURAL DISASTERS

When nature overpowers, engulfs, destroys,
When silence cries and all hope is eclipsed,
When sun is black and faith is a quicksand;
When no stars dance and everywhere
Is dark distress,
May all who witness, all who brave, all those
Who suffer earthquake, tidal wave and fire,
Still hold Your hand,
Still hold Your Spirit close.

A GRACE FOR THOSE WHO LOOK FOR FAITH

May we have the grace to follow St. Paul
Whose faith led him to write:
I am persuaded, that neither death, nor life,
Nor angels, nor principalities,
Nor powers, nor things present,
Nor things to come,
Nor height, nor depth, nor any other creature,
Shall be able to separate us
From the love of God.

A GRACE FOR WAKING UP

Teach me thy love to know,
That this new light, which now I see,
May both the work and workman show:
Then by a sunne-beam, I will climbe to thee.

A GRACE FOR EVERYTHING

You say grace before meals.
All right.
But I say grace before the play and the opera,
And grace before the concert and pantomime,
And grace before I open a book,
And grace before sketching, painting,
Swimming, fencing, boxing, walking,
playing, dancing;
And grace before I dip the pen in the ink.

THE WORLD
IS SO FULL
OF A NUM-
BER OF
THINGS
I THINK WE
SHOULD ALL
BE AS HAPPY
AS KINGS
R.L.STEVENSON

A GRACE FOR FRIENDS

May we have the grace and the love
Not to be fair weather friends,
But when a friend is in pain to share the pain
Even when we have nothing to offer except
our presence,
Even when being there is painful to ourselves.

WE ARE YOUR SHELTER IN THE RAIN

A GRACE FOR SUPERMARKET SHOPPERS

May the grace of calmness fall
On supermarket shoppers; all
Who hurry round yet find they choose
Checkouts with the slowest queues.
Whose trolleys take them for a ride
With wheels that veer from side to side.
Who walk for miles to make up meals
Until their mind and body reels.
And who forget the very thing
They came for and yet buy a string
Of items they cannot afford.
O grant the shopper calmness, Lord.

A GRACE FOR SCHOOLS

This is our school,
Let peace dwell here,
Let the room be full of contentment.
Let love abide here.
Love of one another,
Love of mankind,
Love of life itself,
And love of God.
Let us remember
That as many hands build a house,
So many hearts make a school.

A GRACE FOR AGNOSTICS

Whatever it is that drives things on,
Blind energy, sentient being
Or entity inconceivable by the earthbound,
We thank it for life
And the strength to enjoy it.
We thank it for pain
And the power to feel it,
(For numbness is death.)
We are suitably grateful.
Couldn't it, once in a while,
Nudge a little luck in our direction?

A GRACE FOR THE UNHAPPY

God, Thou art the only hope of the world,
  The only refuge for the unhappy.
  Abiding in the faithfulness of heaven,
Give me strong succour in this testing place.

A GRACE FOR EVERY DAY

G od
Grant me
the Serenity
to accept the things
I cannot change,
Courage
to change
the things I can
and Wisdom
to know
the difference.

A GRACE FOR PEOPLE WITH PROBLEMS

Be patient towards all that is
Unsolved in your heart.
Try to love the questions themselves.
Do not seek the answers
Until you can live the questions,
For the point is to live everything.
Then gradually, without being aware of it,
You may live along some distant day
Into the answers.

A GRACE FOR NEWBORN BABIES

M ay the Lord bless you with all good
And keep you from all evil.
May He give light to your heart with loving wisdom
And be gracious to you with eternal knowledge.
May He lift up his loving countenance upon you
For eternal peace.

A GRACE FOR SLEEPERS

May the angels watch me
As I lie down to sleep.
May angels guard me
As I sleep alone.

A GRACE FOR TODAY'S KNIGHTS IN SHINING ARMOUR

God be in my head
And in my understanding;
God be in mine eyes
And in my looking;
God be in my mouth
And in my speaking;
God be in my heart
And in my thinking;
God be at my end
And at my departing.

Knights in shining armour

A GRACE FOR THOSE WHO NEED PROTECTION

May I arise today
Through God's strength to pilot me:
God's might to uphold me,
God's wisdom to guide me,
God's eye to look before me,
God's ear to hear me,
God's word to speak to me,
God's hand to guard me,
God's way to lie before me,
God's shield to protect me.

A GRACE FOR OLDER PEOPLE

May the right hand of the Lord
Keep us ever in old age,
The Grace of Christ continually defend us
From the enemy.
O Lord direct our heart
In the way of peace.

A GRACE FOR THOSE WHO ARE TEMPTED

Dear Lord and Father of mankind
Forgive our foolish ways!
Re-clothe us in our rightful mind,
In purer lives thy service find,
In deeper reverence praise.
Breathe through the heats of our desire
Thy coolness and thy balm;
Let sense be dumb, let flesh retire;
Speak through the earthquake, wind and fire,
O still small voice of calm.

A GRACE FOR THOSE WHO MOURN

Father of all mercies and giver of comfort
Deal graciously, we pray thee,
with those who mourn,
that casting every care on thee,
they may know the consolation of thy love.

A GRACE FOR REFUGEES

Does the road
Wind uphill all the way?
Yes, to the very end.
Will the day's journey
Take the whole long day?
From morn to night, my friend.
Shall I find comfort,
Travel-sore and weak?
Of labour you shall find the sum.
Will there be beds
For me and all who seek?
Yea, beds for all who come.

A GRACE FOR GARDENERS

There is no plant in the ground
But is full of His virtue,
There is no form in the land
But is full of His blessing.
May all who dig, weed, sow,
All who make gardens,
Praise the Lord and know
They nurture His Creation.

A GRACE FOR THOSE WHO DIED IN BATTLE

Look how many of them there were.
Look how young they were.
They died for our freedom.
Let us hold back our tears
And keep silent.
Lord, may we grace their death
With our remembrance.

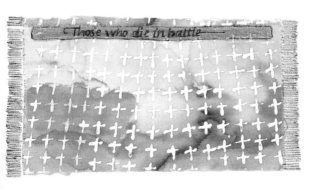

A GRACE FOR ALL NEGOTIATORS

Lord, make me an instrument of Thy peace;
Where there is hatred, let me sow love;
Where there is injury, pardon;
Where there is doubt, faith;
Where there is despair, hope;
Where there is darkness, light;
And where there is sadness, joy.

A GRACE FOR THE DEPRESSED AND ALIENATED

Open our eyes, Lord,
to see your glory;
Open our ears, Lord,
To hear your call;
Open our lips, Lord,
To sing your praises.
Then guide us on our pilgrimage of faith.

A GRACE FOR SINGLE MOTHERS

Mother of our mother,
Guide our hands in yours,
Remind us how
To kindle the hearth,
To keep it bright,
To preserve the flame.
Your hands upon ours,
Our hands within yours
To kindle the light
Both day and night.

A GRACE FOR EVERY KIND OF STUDENT

Lord, since the first task of the mind
Must be to know itself,
Help me to understand my work
And through my work, myself.

A GRACE FOR CARERS

Come unto me all ye that labour
And are heavy laden,
And I will give you rest.
Take my yoke upon you,
And learn of me.
For I am meek and lowly in heart:
And ye shall find rest unto your souls.
For my yoke is easy, and my burden light.

A GRACE FOR WRITERS

Writers everywhere -
May you write
With more than your fingers and hands.
May you use your heart and your soul
So that all your writing,
However big, however small,
May be touched with grace.

A GRACE FOR DRIVERS

Give me the Grace, Lord, not to rue
The others in a traffic queue.
Or rage at those who, just for fun
Drive past like bullets from a gun.
Be near me when I scratch or dent
Or smash my car by accident.
Help me, when I am sorely tried
To visualise a countryside
Where quiet cows graze unaware
And I like them, may stand and stare.

A GRACE FOR THOSE WHO FIND
LIFE DIFFICULT

Give me a mind that is not bored,
That does not whimper, whine or sigh.
Don't let me worry overmuch
About the fussy thing called 'I'.
Give me a sense of humour, Lord,
Give me the Grace to see a joke,
To get some happiness from life
And pass it on to other folk.

A GRACE FOR COOKS

For food and drink and happy days
Accept our gratitude and praise.
In serving others, Lord, we do
Express our thankfulness to you.

A GRACE FOR HOSPITAL WORKERS, PATIENTS AND VISITORS

O God, make the door of this house wide enough
To receive all who need
Human love and fellowship,
And a heavenly Father's care,
And narrow enough to shut out
All envy, pride and hate.
Make it a gateway
To thine eternal kingdom.

A GRACE FOR THE OVER-STRETCHED

Of what use is this restless, hurrying activity?
This heavyweight of earthly duties?
God's purposes stand firm,
And thou, His little one,
Needest one thing alone,
Trust in His power and will, to meet thy need.
God beareth all thy care.

A GRACE BEFORE MEALS

For all the lovely fruits of earth,
For milk that feeds us from our birth.
For fields of grain from which we may
Make bread and rice for every day.
For picnics, pastas, puppodums
For Sunday lunch at Dad and Mum's,
For fish and chip and burger days,
And all the other takeaways,
For meals at home and special treats
(When everybody overeats),
May we always praise you, Lord,
May we always share our food.

A GRACE FOR ALL CREATURES

To all the humble beasts there be,
To all the birds on land and sea,
Great Spirit, sweet protection give
That free and happy they may live!

And to our hearts the rapture bring
Of love for every living thing;
Make us all one kin, and bless
Our ways with Christ's own gentleness!

A GRACE FOR ALL SEA TRAVELLERS

Dear God, be good to me:
The sea is so wide
And my boat is so small.

A GRACE FOR A MEDITATION GROUP

They that wait upon the Lord shall renew
their strength.
They shall mount up with wings as eagles;
They shall run, and not be weary; And they shall
walk and not faint.

A GRACE FOR SPINNERS, WEAVERS AND DYERS

God loveth Sinners,
Dyers and Spinners.
Weavers even
May hope for Heaven.
When nought is left
Of warp and weft
With spindle and loom
They will meet their doom.
The Lamb's white fleece
Has bought their peace.

A GRACE FOR ALL WORKERS

Lord may we remember
That every man and woman should eat and drink
And enjoy the good of all their labour.
It is the gift of God.

A GRACE FOR EVERY MEMBER OF A FAMILY

To every thing there is a season,
And a time to every purpose under the heaven:
A time to be born, and a time to die.
A time to plant, and a time to pluck up that
which is planted.
A time to kill, and a time to heal,
A time to break down and a time to build up.
A time to weep and a time to laugh.
A time to mourn, and a time to dance.
A time to cast away stones, and a time to gather
stones together. . .

A GRACE FOR THOSE WHO WANT TO GIVE UP

Lord, let us have the grace to remember.
We are all the children of light, and the children of
the day: we are not of the night, nor of darkness.
Therefore let us not sleep, as others do; but let us
watch and be sober. For they that sleep, sleep in the
night; and they that be drunken are drunken in the
night. But let us, who are of the day, be sober,
putting on the breastplate of faith and love; and for a
helmet, the hope of salvation.

the breast plate of faith

A GRACE FOR CONVALESCENTS

Let quietness and confidence
Be your strength.
In rest and returning
You shall be saved, secured, released.

A GRACE FOR HOSTS AND HOSTESSES

Be not forgetful to entertain strangers: for
therby some
have entertained angels unawares.

good heavens above!

A GRACE FOR TIMES OF FAILURE

The leaves are falling, falling as from far,
As though above were withering farthest gardens;
They fall with a denying attitude.
And night by night, down into solitude,
The heavy earth falls far from every star.
We are all falling. This hand's falling too –
All have this falling sickness, non withstands.
And yet there's One whose gently folding hands
This universal falling can't fall through.

A GRACE FOR PESSIMISTS

Whatsoever things are true, whatsoever things
are honest, whatsoever
Things are just, whatsoever things are pure,
whatsoever things are lovely,
Whatsoever things are of good report;
If there be any virtue and if there be any praise,
Think on these things.

A GRACE FOR THOSE WHO HATE GOING
TO THE DENTIST

Lord when I'm in the dentist's chair
Help me relax without a care.
And when the dentist pricks my gums
So every nerve vibrates and hums.
And when he switches on his drill
So I think: 'Is he out to kill?'
(Although I know he's very kind,)
Lord give me a still, rational mind.

A GRACE FOR THOSE WHO ARE
MADE REDUNDANT

Lives of great men all remind us
We can make our lives sublime.
And departing leave behind us
Footprints on the sand of time.

Let us then be up and doing
With a heart for any fate.
Still achieving, still pursuing,
Learn to labour and to wait.

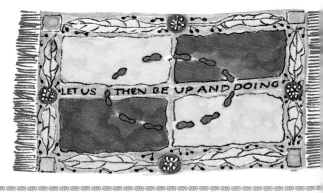

A GRACE FOR COLD AND HUNGRY CHILDREN

Here a little child I stand,
Heaving up my either hand,
Cold as paddocks* though they be,
Here I lift them up to Thee,
For a benison** to fall
On our meat, and on us all.

A GRACE FOR GOLFERS

For drives that soar
For chips that hold;
For putts that drop
When twice too bold;
For food and friends
On golfing days;
To God we give

Our thanks and praise.

A GRACE FOR THE NEW YEAR

No east, no west.
Snow conceals the past.

The old year dreams
And the snow boy comes

With faith and light
To lead us gently out

Where we must go
Across the unmarked snow.

INDEX